Who Are You?

Who Are You?

Reclaiming Your Identity In Christ

BY PASTOR DON E. GERMAN

XULON PRESS

Xulon Press
2301 Lucien Way #415
Maitland, FL 32751
407.339.4217
www.xulonpress.com

Pastor Don E. German is the Senior Pastor of Interdenomination of Faith Church of the Living God – Columbus, GA Inc. The ministry is associated and covered by Bishop Thomas and Prophetess Josephine Urquhart, Interdenomination of Faith Church of the Living God, Inc. in Leesville, Louisiana.

Pastor German is a retired Army Chaplain retiring from Fort Benning, GA in 2010. During his 29 years and 3 months on Active Duty he has held various positions within the Army Chaplaincy culminating at the rank of Lieutenant Colonel, Deputy Garrison Chaplain and Pastor of the Sightseeing Road Gospel Service. IDF-Columbus began at the Pastor's house in September of 2008 and in October 2008 officially became a church. On January 11, 2009 IDF-Columbus held its first service at the Salvation Army Worship and Community Center, 5201 Warm Springs Road in Columbus. The church presently worships at 3127 Tower Road, Bldg. B, in Columbus, GA.

Pastor German leads IDF-Columbus with a passion for the Word of God and compassion for the people of God! The church's Vision reflects the personality of Pastor German: Vision: *CHRISTIANS WHO ARE WHOLE, PURE, SPIRIT-FILLED AND EXCITED ABOUT THE THINGS OF GOD!*

Pastor German is a graduate of Clemson University, Clemson, SC, graduating with a Bachelor of Science Degree in Recreation and Parks Administration. He is also a graduate, Magna Cum Laude, School of Theology Virginia Union University, Richmond, VA, graduating with a Masters of Divinity degree. Pastor German has served in the education system at the Chattahoochee County Middle and High School as their In School

Suspension teacher during the 2010-2011 school year. From July 2011-June 2014, Pastor German taught at Americus Sumter High School in Americus, GA as the Senior Army Instructor of their JROTC Program. Presently, he is the Junior Leadership Corps instructor at Baker Middle School in Columbus, GA.

Pastor German is married to Co-Pastor Annell German for the past 35 years and currently resides in Columbus, GA. They have two adult children, Dana Elizabeth, Leesville, LA, a clinician working with Autistic children in Lake Charles, LA and Daniel Charles, a student at Full Sail University, Orlando, FL.

Indeed this is the Lord's doing and it is marvelous in our eyes.

DEDICATION

This book is dedicated to my parents, Charles and Williemae German, who are now in the presence of our Heavenly Father! Thank you, daddy and mommy, for being the first to help me to answer the question "Who Are You?" Through their nurturing as loving parents I realized that the Lord was teaching me through them about who I am! It first started with understanding that I am a German – I represent the family name! Most importantly, I belong to Charles and Williemae German! My parents had a good reputation in the community of Mt. Pleasant, SC. I affectionately called them the "king and queen" of Mt.

Pleasant! I love my parents and I can say today I am who I am because of who they were – they loved the Lord God and served Him with a whole heart!

Dedicated to my big brother Carlos, known to the art world as Arnold C. German who prepared the cover for this book and who I plan to ask to do all books I write. To my sister Carlotta, who was with both Daddy and Mommy as they transitioned into eternal life! Thank you indeed for your labor of love in caring for them. What you did and went through during that time was absolutely phenomenal and I do appreciate you being there! I have not forgotten, nor has God forgotten what you did!

I also dedicate this book to my loving family! My wife, Annell. Thank you honey for praying for me, sticking it out with me not only in this project, but also our lives that we have shared together thus far! This ride is far from over and I am so glad that you are right by my side to accompany me on the journey to come!

My adult children, Dana and Daniel! You two are the best! I am so privileged to be your father! I am so proud of you both in all that you have accomplished in your life and I know that the best is yet to come! Thank you for loving the Lord Jesus Christ and putting your full trust in HIM! Thank you indeed for loving your daddy even when church, work, and being a pastor took me away from spending more time together.

So many others in my life that have played a significant role in knowing who I am in Christ Jesus! My pastors and overseer, Bishop Thomas and Prophetess Josephine Urquhart, Interdenomination of Faith Church of the Living God - Louisiana. Thank you, Bishop and Prophetess for nurturing, mentoring, giving sage wise Godly counsel in helping Annell and me to be the pastors we are today. To Apostle Gregory Ransaw, Founder of Covenant Partners Ministry of Killen, TX, who have inspired me in so many ways and reminds me of words that I have spoken! Thank you, Apostle for your constant support and encouragement you have given to me since the time the Lord knitted us together.

To the congregation of Interdenomination of Faith Church of the Living God – Columbus, GA! You have been such a blessing to me and my family and I thank you for your support, love, and encouragement. This book is dedicated to you as well! How I love you all!

ACKNOWLEDGEMENTS

$\mathcal{J}$t is with sincere appreciation that I acknowledge those of who I owe a debt of gratitude for the completion of this book. Without their help, you would have seen a lot of grammatical errors, misspelled words, and incomplete sentences! Thank you Annell and Minister Althea Brown for taking the time to be new eyes to read what I wrote! And Evangelist Tonya Samuels in helping with the rework of the chapter "Be Anxious for Nothing."

Arnold C. German, my brother who designed the front cover of the book! Thank you big brother. Your drawings are amazing! I have always admired your paintings!

I thank Minister (Mother) Sheila Downs for praying with Annell and me when we laid the final draft on the altar presenting it to the Lord for HIS service and HIS glory!

I acknowledge Holy Spirit in leading me to write the book and edging me on to get it done! Thank you Lord for you have done great and mighty things!

To all that is happening and all that will take place from here on out, I say, TO GOD BE THE GLORY GREAT THINGS HE HAS DONE, IS DOING, AND WILL DO! Thank you, Lord!

TABLE OF CONTENTS

Introduction xix

Our Identity from the Beginning 1

Identity Theft in the Garden 13

The Plan of God Never Changed 20

Be Anxious for Nothing 26

The Enemy's Plotting Against You 37

False Identity 52

Who Are You? This is Who You Are 62

Conclusion 103

Who Are You?
INTRODUCTION

*D*o you know who you are? I am not talking about that you know your name and family tree. I am talking about do you know that you are spirit, one that has come from God. The enemy also known as Satan, the devil, the evil one, desires to keep you from knowing your true identity! If the enemy can keep you from knowing who you are, then you will lose and miss all that belongs to you. This is the strategy of the enemy to keep you from knowing who you are in the Lord, Satan intends to steal your identity and gather everything that belongs to you.

In the 21st century there is this growing crime call "Identity Theft". The problem is so great that many companies have devoted themselves to assisting the victims of this crime. Books have been written on the subject. Mr. Michael McCoy and Steffen Schmidt, PhD authors of the book THE SILENT CRIME, published by Twin Lakes Press in 2008 wrote,

"As we completed our book Who is You? The Coming Epidemic of Identity Theft several years ago the following news story had just broken: This June, when news broke that 40 million Master Cards had been hacked, was one of the most discouraging days in recent memory .... We did not know at that time that things would go steeply downhill from there. Most of what was being written two years ago said, "Everything is under control. Don't worry. Move on. All is being taken care

of. The government will come to the rescue"
or something to that effect. How wrong
they were! Time Magazine wrote in its first
January, 2008 issue, "162 million" "Number
of personal-data records affected in security
breaches reported by 302 organizations in
2007"....(pg. 1,2)

Now that's in the natural world of the problem with
identity theft. McCoy and Schmidt defines identity
theft in this way: Identity theft occurs when someone
possesses or uses your name, address, Social Security
number, bank or credit card number, or other identi-
fying information without your knowledge with the
intent to commit fraud or other crimes." In the spiritual sense the enemy has been stealing the identity of
the people of God ever since the fall in the Garden of
Eden. Satan has been committing a fraud against the
creation of God and has stolen the kingdom through

deception and deceit but the real problem is actually the people of God being careless and having a case of amnesia of who they are in Christ! It is not that Satan stole the kingdom, Adam gave it away because Adam forgot what his Creator called him to be. This is what Adam gave away to Satan:

26 And God said, ...let them have dominion... over all the earth .... 28 And God blessed them, and God said unto them, Be fruitful, and multiply, and replenish the earth, and subdue it: and have dominion ... upon the earth." Genesis 1:26;28 (KJV)

The purpose of this book is to assist you to reclaim your identity! Just as there are companies out in the world to assist you from the "silent crime" you will have assistance from this book and from THE BOOK, THE B-I-B-L-E, Basic Instruction Before Leaving

Earth, to realize your identity in Christ Jesus! The Lord has indeed given us HIS WORD and directions to reclaim our identity and therefore fulfill our kingdom mandate to take dominion on this earth!

In order for you and I to fulfill this Kingdom Mandate, we must insure that we know who we are in this world! I remember watching the *Lion King* (*The Lion King*. Dirs. Rob Minkoff, Roger Allers. Perfs. James Earl Jones, Jeremy Irons, Jonathan Taylor Thomas. Walt Disney Pictures, 1994. DVD.) and God gave me revelation of how the enemy uses lies, deception, and deceit to steal the identity of those called out of darkness. In the *Lion King* Simba was the heir to the throne to take Mufasa's (the present king) place because of his position as son to Mufasa. Scar the brother to Mufasa was next in line because Mufasa at the time did not have a son, but the moment Simba was born, Scar was taken out of the picture. The enemy has always wanted to be worshipped and desired the kingdom but he is not in line to receive the Kingdom – only those who are sons and daughters. The following passage lets us know who are the sons and daughters. John 1: 12 (KJV), *"But as many as received him, to them gave he power to become the sons of God, even to them that believe on his name...."* and Romans 8:17 (ERV) *"If we are God's children, we will get the blessings God has for his people. He will give us all that he has given Christ...."* It is up to the daughters and sons of God to remember and know who they are in order to possess what is rightfully theirs. When we don't know who we are then we miss out and cannot or will not obtain what God has ordained to be ours!

Of course the enemy will have his role to play in the scheme of things. Just like the one who desires to get your stuff or use your name for their own personal gain, the enemy plots and schemes to attack your identity and tell you all sorts of lies to obtain, steal what the LORD has for you! Scar plotted to have his brother killed and put the blame on Simba accusing Simba of the death of his father, suggesting the best thing for him to do is to run away and never come back! Well of course once the heir to the throne is no longer there to take the throne the kingdom needs a leader, which Scar graciously accepts and leads the Pride Land into ruins. In the meantime, Simba is out, left for dead in the desert. This is how the enemy will treat you in cheating you from the kingdom! The enemy does not want you to walk into your destiny! The enemy knows that what God has for you is awesome, so therefore he, will deceive, lie, cheat, steal to keep you from your blessings. John 10:10a tells us: *"The thief does not come except to steal, and to kill, and to destroy...."*

The enemy will come after you! That is why is it vitally important that you know who you are in Christ Jesus! When Simba was out there in the wilderness all wrapped up in guilt and shame and as the days passed by was convinced by Pumbaa, a wart hog and

Timon, a meerkat, that he is in a new world and that he needed to forget about his past and live life new, changing his ways, especially his eating habits! Now here's a lion being convinced that he no longer likes meat, but to subject himself to worms, grubs, and bugs! Pumbaa and Timon should have been Simba's lunch. Things however, began to change when Nala, Simba's lioness friend he grew up with was on the hunt for food, attacked Pumbaa, but Simba jumps in to protect Pumbaa and the two lions fight and Simba recognizes her and calls her name and she steps back and asked the most intriguing, yet simple question: "Who are you?" He reveals his identity and immediately Nala asked the question, what are you doing here, we all thought that you were dead! Later in the movie, Rafiki, the spiritual leader says to him, "…you don't know who you are!" Friends, I believe this is what the Lord is saying to us when we are not acting according to who we are in Christ Jesus! Who are you? You don't know who you are! Also, as Mufasa comes to Simba in the clouds, and states, "Simba, you have forgotten me – you have forgotten that I said I will be with you always." This is what the Lord is saying to us today as he said it to Joshua, *"I will never leave you, nor forsake you." Joshua 1:5b (GWT).*

We must all realize that as we come into the truth of the Word of God, please note that the enemy is just not going to lay down without a fight! The scripture tells us that the **kingdom of heaven has suffered violence, and the violent take it by force! Matthew 11:12 (ESV).** The enemy is not going to just let you take it, but the enemy will mount up a great defense against you. Knowing who you are in Christ Jesus, you will recall what Jesus said, *"…In the world you will have tribulation; but be of good cheer, I have overcome the world." John 16:33b (NKJV).* And again, the Apostle John shares, *"You are of God, little children, and have overcome them, because He who is in you is greater than he* *who is in the world." I John 4:4 (NKJV).* Victory is already ours through the redemptive work of JESUS CHRIST! HE won when HE died on the cross and rose triumphantly over death and the grave! JESUS has redeemed us from the curse and has set us free. All those who believe and receive HIM as their Lord and Savior, have an inheritance, the truth, and HE has set you free! Go forth and claim what is yours!

Who are you? This question has eternal consequences in how you answer! Depending on your answer, you can be eternally blessed with the understanding of who you are in Christ Jesus or you can be eternally bankrupt by missing out on the blessings of GOD simply because you do not know who you are! No one can answer this question for you. You must answer for yourself! Go with me on this journey to answer the question, **Who Are You?**

OUR IDENTITY FROM THE BEGINNING

"And God said, Let us make man in our image,
after our likeness: and let them have dominion ...."
Genesis 1:26a (NKJV)

When we were born into this world we didn't have a clue of what was on the inside of us! Other people as we grow up, will make some predictions of what our future might be based on what they observe! God has placed in all of us to be whatever we choose to be! He has placed in us greatness! I say greatness because God did not make junk when

1

He created you and I! The scripture says in Psalms 139:14 (NKJV), *I will praise You, for I am fearfully and wonderfully made; Marvelous are Your works, And that my soul knows very well.* Psalms 139:16 (NLT) says: *"You saw me before I was born. Every day of my life was recorded in your book. Every moment was laid out before a single day had passed".* Psalm 139: 16 (MSG), says it this way: *"Like an open book, you watched me grow from conception to birth; all the stages of my life were spread out before you, the days of my life all prepared before I'd even lived one day."*

I can remember in my life as I was growing up that some of my relatives predicted that I would become a preacher! Some said it because I loved fried chicken! It has been said that chicken is the "gospel bird" of the church and the number one meat for all preachers! Others saw something in me and therefore spoke it over me, even when I did not see myself as a preacher!

2

An interesting thing took place in my life, the more I heard it, and I began to think on it – my life had a tendency to go toward it! I felt the tugging of my heart towards spiritual things as I attended Sunday School and church. I was a typical kid growing up! I don't know of any young person who has not at one time or another been disobedient to their parents. There may be some out there, but I was not one of them. I learned early in my growing up, that obedience was so much better than rebelling!   By the way, my parents had a remedy for disobedience and rebellion – The BELT! Yes, I got my share of spankings and whippings! As I look back over those times, I realize now that God used my parents to shape and form my heart to be obedient and respect authority! I thank God for my parents who showed love towards me by not allowing me to continue in my rebellion and disobedience. What was happening in my life is that God was using my parents and others who took an interest in my well-being, by putting a demand on the potential that was locked up on the inside of me! Potential that GOD placed in me!

That discipline that I received from my parents and others was for my good! At the time of the discipline I did not think so but my parents and others saw the potential in me to do great things and had the guidance of the LORD to ensure that I was disciplined when I would stray off the path to help me to understand that doing the right thing will keep me out of trouble and therefore keep me on the right path to my destiny – to my expected end.

Jeremiah 29:11 is for all who would put their trust in the LORD. I like how the King James Version reads: *"For I know the thoughts that I think toward you, saith the LORD, thoughts of peace, and not of evil, to give you an expected end."* This lets me know that the Lord has given us all potential to do something great in the Kingdom! Potential as an adjective means *possible, as opposed to actual or capable of being or becoming*. As a noun it means a latent excellence or ability that may or may not be developed. The latter part of the definition is so very important for it says, "… Ability that may or may not be developed." You see if the potential on the inside is not developed it does not mean that it was never there! You and I, God's creation, have always had "potential" to do whatever it is that comes to mind – it must be developed! It is up to the person to develop that potential on the inside.

I heard Dr. Bill Winston, founder and senior pastor of Living Word Christian Center of Chicago, IL, say this about potential. He said, in order for the potential on the inside of you come out or develop, a demand must be placed on that potential in order for it to manifest or be seen! I interpret that to mean that life has a way of supplying that demand! I don't know if you have noticed but life is demanding! There have been many things in which if it wasn't for the demand – if it wasn't for the pressures of life – I would have never known what I was capable of doing! Although at times I thought it was going to "kill me" but instead it developed me into the person I am today! When a person is first confronted with the Gospel of Jesus Christ there is a demand being placed on you because now you must consider the ways of the Word of God that you have been introduced to and compare it with the life you have without Christ. You must now make a decision to accept or reject the message you heard! Even in reading this book, a demand is being placed on you in answering the basic question, "Who Are You?" The sole purpose of this book is to help you to come back to your true identity of who you are in Christ Jesus! There is not a person living on this earth that was saved from day one of their existence. The Word lets us know in Romans 3:10-12, from the NKJV, *"As it is written: "There is none righteous, no, not one; There is none who understands; There is none who seeks after God. They have all turned aside; They have together become unprofitable; There is none who does good, no, not one."* And again in verse 23, *"for all have sinned and fall short of the glory of God.* It is because of my predicament as described in those verses I had to look beyond myself and make a confession of faith to trust Jesus Christ as my savior. *But God demonstrates His own love toward us, in that while we were still sinners, Christ died for us. (Romans 5:8) and in Chapter 6 verse 23, "For the wages of sin is death, but the gift of God is eternal life in Christ Jesus our Lord.* Praise the Lord, because of this confrontation with this "good news" the demand and the decision made to follow Christ begins the journey of finding out who I really am, who I was created to be as ordained by the Creator! My spirit can now pursue with understanding who I am! I can now identify with my Creator. With Jesus Christ in my life, I have positioned myself to see the potential in me having placed my trust in the LORD. I am a firm believer in knowing that Jesus Christ makes all the difference in the world. That is why I need to develop my relationship with Him! I need to spend time with the Lord – get focus and stay focus on Him. When the Apostle Peter asked Jesus to walk on water, Jesus gave a most profound response: "COME!" And with that invitation, Peter walked on water as long as he kept his eyes on Jesus! The Bible tells us that when he took his eyes off of Jesus and focused more on the winds and waves it was only then that he began to sink but bless the LORD, Peter remembered who he asked in the first place to come out on the water – *"… and beginning to sink he cried out, saying, "Lord, save me!" And immediately Jesus stretched out His hand and caught him, and said to him, "O you of little faith, why did you doubt?" Matthew 14: 30B-31 (NKJV).*

Adam and Eve had their identity in God from the very beginning. The LORD gave them their Kingdom Identity and entrusted them with this Kingdom Mandate found in Genesis 1:26-28 (KJV):

8

And God said, Let us make man in our image, after our likeness: and let them have dominion over the fish of the sea, and over the fowl of the air, and over the cattle, and over all the earth, and over every creeping thing that creepeth upon the earth. 27 So God created man in his *own* image, in the image of God created he him; male and female created he them. 28 And God blessed them, and God said unto them, Be fruitful, and multiply, and replenish the earth, and subdue it: and have dominion over the fish of the sea, and over the fowl of the air, and over every living thing that moveth upon the earth.

Did you catch the Kingdom Identity? *"And God said, Let us make man in our image, after our like-ness:... So God created man in his own image, in the*

9

image of God created he him; male and female created he them." You see from the very beginning of time when God created Adam and Eve, He gave them their identity. Genesis 2:7 completes Genesis 1:26a and 27 in that God gave life to that identity -- *"And the Lord God made the man of the dust of the ground, and breathed into his nostrils the breath of life; and <u>MAN BECAME A LIVING BEING."</u> [Emphasis mine]*.

Now, my friends that should get you excited and truly get you started in knowing that when God formed you in your mother's womb, HE formed you and I from good stuff, awesome ingredients, our true identity – "the image and likeness of God! My brother in the Lord, Ralph Jones, in a Bible Study night truly captured the definition of our true identity when he stated, *"We are living breathing representations of God!"* I really rejoiced over his statement because I know that flesh and blood did not reveal that to Brother Ralph, but the Spirit of the Almighty God! LIVING

BREATHING REPRESENTATIONS OF GOD! This is our true identity!

The Kingdom Mandate comes right on the heels of our Kingdom Identity! The mandate is for His creation to have dominion: *and let them have dominion over the fish of the sea, and over the fowl of the air, and over the cattle, and over all the earth, and over every creeping thing that creepeth upon the earth.* From the book "KINGDOM PRINCIPLES" by Dr. Myles Munroe he wrote , *"The mandate of the Creator for mankind was rulership and dominion.... "dominion" here translate ... meaning "kingdom" or "sovereign rule" or government. Therefore, the first command given to man by his Creator was to establish a "government" on the earth to destroy chaos and to maintain order. Government is God's solution to disorder."* Please take note that our KINGDOM MANDATE is to have dominion over nature, the animal world, this physical world! NOT OVER EACH OTHER! For I believe as we come under the PROTECTION of the LORD, looking to HIM to guide and direct our "rulership" our taking dominion, we would live together in harmony! Only as we stay in fellowship with our CREATOR! Only as we build our relationship with the LORD, walk with HIM, talk with HIM, be like HIM, look like HIM, act like HIM can we indeed fulfill this Kingdom Mandate! Something happen that robbed Adam and Eve and the entire human race of their Kingdom Identity! Identity theft took place in the Garden of Eden.

IDENTITY THEFT IN
THE GARDEN

Now the serpent was more cunning than any beast
of the field which the Lord God had made. And he
said to the woman, ..." Genesis 3:1 (NKJV)

*B*ut something happen in the garden. Something
happen in paradise. Something took place that
stripped Adam and Eve, actually cheated them out of
their blessing – which had tremendous consequences
on the entire human race. Some people may think that
personal sins only affect that individual person, but no,
no, it's not even about you. Your decisions affect all

those around you and that which is on the inside of you – the SPIRIT of GOD. The decision that Adam and Eve made to disobey God in His one command to Adam: *And the Lord God commanded the man, saying, "Of every tree of the garden you may freely eat; but of the tree of the knowledge of good and evil you shall not eat, for in the day that you eat of it you shall surely die." Genesis 2:16-17 (NKJV)* was the first identity theft in the history of mankind! Read the account of how the serpent indeed slithered its way into the lives of Adam and Eve. The enemy's tactic is always to question God's commands and to make us think that God is holding out on us. Also, the enemy would want us to think that obedience to the Lord's command and Word is not necessary or that they are merely suggestions! *Has God indeed said, … You shall not surely die. For God knows that in the day you eat of it your eyes will be opened, and you will be like God, knowing good and evil." Genesis 3:1, 4-5 (NKJV).*

Eve fell for the deception and instead of standing on what she received from Adam not to eat from the tree, saw that the tree was good, pleasant, and desirable to make one wise, ate from the tree and one who should have halted the entire proceeding, the head, the priest of the home, the one that got the command directly from God Adam, was with Eve when the entire conversation was taking place with the serpent. Instead of Adam stepping in and taking dominion in this situation with what was already given to him in Genesis 1:26, Adam allowed his identity to be taken from him. He gave up his position in the Kingdom to now, when they heard the Lord in the garden, instead of going to Him and having fellowship, they hid themselves, realizing they were naked! Friends, this is what happens when we disobey the Lord! We don't run to him, but there is a tendency to want to hide and not be in the presence of Truth! I know when I did something wrong, I did not want to be in the presence of my parents because

I knew that meant some kind of punishment! I recall in my marriage having made a financial decision but I did not consult with my wife and later she confronted me and I lied about it. My wife accepted my word, but I knew that I had lied and believe you me it was not a comfortable feeling being in her presence, let alone Holy Spirit on the inside of me just wearing me out. Days later I told my wife that I lied and she forgave me. The point I am making is that when you do wrong you don't want to be in the presence of those walking up right with the Lord, or you don't want to have quiet time with the Lord!

You may be reading and it occurs to you that you don't know who you are or who you can be. It could be because you have listened to the wrong voice. You were in a conversation with the enemy and he has deceived you into thinking that you don't need to obey the command of God! You have listened to voices that will keep you away from having the very best of

God. Some of you have fallen prey to the deceiver, who comes and cheats you out of the blessings of God and convinces you that God is holding back on you – to doubt what God has said namely, *"be fruitful and multiply…of every tree of the garden you may freely eat …fill the earth and subdue it … have dominion.* The enemy speaks to your flesh – speaks to the dust – speaks to that part of you that is nothing – speaks sweet nothings in your ear -- all for a cheap little, five to ten minutes of so call pleasure -- and I'm not just talking about sex, but also taking that drink or smoke or hit or pill, or telling that lie, knowing that it is wrong. Worst of all simply disobeying what God has said or directed you to do or not to do! I don't know how long the conversation went on between the devil, Eve, and Adam but when you spend more time talking to the enemy the results will be that you begin to follow your own passions. ***You are tempted by the evil things you want. Your own desire leads you away and traps you.*[15]*Your*** *desire grows inside you until it results in sin. Then the sin grows bigger and bigger and finally ends in death. James 1:15-16 (ERV).*

From Adam and Eve's decision to disobey brought forth sin into the world in that all who were born of a woman were born into sin -- *Behold, I was brought forth in iniquity, And in sin my mother conceived me. Psalms 51:5 (NKJV).* So we can see from Adam and Eve's decision that it just did not affect them but all who would come after them! As a matter of fact, in the next chapter, Chapter 4, from this interruption, we find Cain killing his brother Abel because of jealousy and selfishness! Friends know that your disobedience, your sin does not just affect you, but it will touch others in some way, shape, form, or fashion.

What happen to our identity? It was cunningly stolen by the serpent who through crafty and convincing words ambushed Adam and Eve into thinking that God was holding out on them and keeping them from being like God! Adam and Eve should have realized that they had everything they needed (Genesis 1:28-30; 2:9-16), and were already created in the image and likeness of God (Genesis 1:26-28, 2:7)! Adam and Eve's decision sent the entire human race in a downward spiral, in essence a spiritual death that the Lord said would happen, *"... for in the day that you eat of it you shall surely die." Genesis 2:17b (NKJV).*

Friends let me remind you that our disobedience to the Word of God does not bring about the blessings of God! God is not holding out on us but desires for each of us to be blessed beyond our wildest dreams! We too must know that when we are born again, born of the Spirit, we recapture our identity and can now get back to our true identity, our Kingdom Identity and live according to the Word of God! We can become a new creation in Christ Jesus! He will make you brand new!

THE PLAN OF GOD
NEVER CHANGED

And I will give you the keys of the kingdom of heaven, and whatever you bind on earth will be bound in heaven, and whatever you loose on earth will be loosed in heaven." Matthew 16:19 (NKJV)

The awesome discovery I have made in my journey as a child of God is that nothing that I or others do, not even or should I say especially the devil, thwarts the plans of God! Adam and Eve's eyes are now open to good and evil and they have sinned and are now in a state of spiritual death. Though Adam and Eve have sinned before the Lord, God shows from the beginning that His plan of man taking dominion and fulfilling the Kingdom Mandate was placed in the salvation plan. He told the enemy, *"... And I will put enmity between you and the woman, and between your seed and her Seed; He shall bruise your head, and you shall bruise His heel." Genesis 3:15 (NKJV).* Charles Stanley's commentary on this verse from the The Charles F. Stanley Life Principals Bible says, "God has a plan. From the very beginning of time, He moved history toward the Cross—where Christ would restore sinful humans like us to rich fellowship with Himself."

This is good news for those of us who have messed up in life, even after confessing Jesus Christ as Lord and Savior! When we do fall we in our humanity have a tendency to live in condemnation, regret, and depression. The Word of God lets us know that we don't have to go there! 1 John 1:9 states, *God is faithful and reliable. If we confess our sins, he forgives them and cleanses us from everything we've done wrong. (GWT).* And in Romans 8:1-2, *There is therefore now no condemnation to those who are in Christ Jesus, because through Christ Jesus the law of the Spirit who gives life has set you free from the law of sin and death. (NIV).* Look at the love the Lord has for His creation! The Apostle Paul realizes that we serve an awesome and loving God by saying to the Christians in Rome, *But God demonstrates His own love toward us, in that while we were still sinners, Christ died for us. Romans 5:8 (NKJV).* People of God Christ died on the cross for the guilt, shame, sickness, sins, mistakes, bad attitudes, situations, circumstances, problems, depression – HE DIED FOR IT ALL! HE DIED THAT YOU AND I MAY LIVE! What love the Father has for His creation! This is why you or I, nor the devil can stop the plans of God! It is the Father's good pleasure to give us the keys to the kingdom!

The Kingdom Mandate will be manifested! The question is will you be one to bring it to pass? The only way you can be a part of this is that you must answer the question, WHO ARE YOU? If you don't know who you are in Christ Jesus you will not be a part of the Kingdom Mandate! You will not experience in full the blessings of the LORD! Get your identity back!

Every promise that the LORD has made from HIS WORD He will bring it to pass! Again, the question is will you be a part of it! Be reminded you are a child of the king, the SPIRIT of the Living God dwells in you. You will be successful, you will prosper, "be fruitful and multiply...of every tree of the garden you may freely eat ... fill the earth and subdue it ... have dominion." From the very beginning, God wanted us to see and know "who we are" and claim that "which is ours." *"The earth is the LORD's, and all its fullness, The world and those who dwell therein." Psalms 24:1 (NKJV).*

Knowing what happen in the Garden of Eden and having humanity's identity stolen does not deter the plan of God should cause you to rejoice and know that you can reclaim your identity. A lot of identity theft companies out there have protection and claim that they would spend up to million dollars to fight for you to get your identity back! Are you not glad that 2,000 years ago, Christ died on the cross and rose again to assure that your identity will be restored! All we have to do is identify with Him. The Apostle Paul wrote to the believers at Corinth, *"Therefore, if anyone is in Christ, he is a new creation; old things have passed away; behold, all things have become new." II Corinthians 5:17, NKJV.* I really like Charles Stanley's commentary on this verse from his LIFE'S PRINCIPLES BIBLE: *"The new birth experience is exactly what God says it is—a fresh beginning. When we are born again, we not only have our sin forgiven and our guilt removed, but we also receive the Holy*

Spirit—who comes to indwell us and live Christ's life through us. We can never be what we were before because we have been born into His life—with a new spirit and nature. And because of that, our desires and goals should be conformed to those that God has for us." Now this truly excites me because I have fallen since asking Christ to come into my life! I have done wrong! But as I shared earlier, the LORD makes a way every time and welcomes me back and will welcome you with open arms ready to forgive and lead you on to where He desires!

As a child of God, you will recognize that you must fight the good fight of faith! There will be mountains you have to climb! It will not be a bed of roses for you in living your life after you say yes to Christ! Trust God and wait on Him to carry you through the storms of life! Nothing can stop the plans of God, we must indeed wait on HIM!

BE ANXIOUS FOR NOTHING

Don't worry about anything; instead, pray about everything. Tell God what you need, and thank him for all he has done.⁷ Then you will experience God's peace, which exceeds anything we can understand. His peace will guard your hearts and minds as you live in Christ Jesus.

Philippians 4:6,7 (New Living Translation, NLT)

"Don't worry about anything; instead, pray about everything ..." is how the New Living Translation translates Paul's admonition to the church at Philippi and to the followers of Christ today.

26

Unfortunately, in the United States alone over 40 million American adults are affected by anxiety disorders every year. Anxiety disorders target not only adults but teenagers and children as well. In fact, 8% of teens ages 13 to 18 have an anxiety disorder, with symptoms starting around age 6. *(Retrieved from* https://www.womenshealth.gov/a-z *topics/anxiety-disorders).* Anxiety is a feeling of worry, nervousness, or fear about an event or situation. It is a normal reaction to stress, but can be disabling if it interferes with daily life, such as making your dread nonthreatening day-to-day activities. I believe if one knows who they are in Christ and confesses their identity on a daily basis, then the reaction to the stresses of life will not become a factor in keeping them from completing their kingdom assignment in the Kingdom of God!

One of the areas that used to bring great anxiety to me was when it was time to pay the bills. Pay day should have been happy days, but at the end of the

day of paying bills, money would run low fast, therefore bringing me to a place where I began to wonder
how to pay the rest of the bills. Much of my financial
woes were self-inflicted, meaning I made bad financial
choices that put me in the high anxiety arena because
my income was losing the race to what I had to pay out.
However, since then, my focus has shifted to choosing
to know who I am in Christ. I have discovered that
Jesus wants to be my financial advisor! I am learning
to lean and depend on the Lord to lead guide and direct
my financial decisions, thus, eliminating those very
anxieties. With prayer and supplications with thanksgiving and knowing my identity in Christ, I now have
the peace of God that takes me well beyond my understanding, and to know that God has my finances in His
hands. Now I am learning to rest in this very promise,
I just need to follow. Peace now reigns in my life when
it comes to paying bills!

One of the treatments for anxiety disorders is coun-
seling. In Isaiah 9:6 we have this tremendous verse,
A child will be born for us. A son will be given to us.
The government will rest on his shoulders. He will
be named: <u>WONDERFUL COUNSELOR</u>, Mighty
God, Everlasting Father, Prince of Peace. (GWT,
emphasis mine). Now coupled with the exhortation
from Philippians 4:5 not to worry but to pray about
everything is God's way of telling us that you have
the power to indeed speak to your anxieties and live
victoriously. Answering the question who are you by
searching the scriptures you will gain a new perspec-
tive in knowing that you are a new creature in Christ
and will come to understand and know that God has
not given you a spirit of fear:

For God has not given us a spirit of fear, but
of power and of love and of a sound mind. II
Timothy 1:7 (NKJV)

29

Another area that causes anxieties in our lives is dwelling on past mistakes. How many of you at one time or another really got down on yourself because of past mistakes? You find yourself just in a depressed state! Now mind you I am talking about people who are saved, sanctified, Holy Ghost filled, and fire baptized believers who get down and depressed! The reason for this deflation is because of life's situations, life's storms that come up in our lives! And the thing of it all is that no one is immune to it! I believe we all have experienced it in our lives! For me it usually comes when I think about bills, situations at the church, people that I have a love and concern for, jobs, projects – any of those areas! I have discovered that when I do think about these areas and I look within myself, and my own strength to try and solve those situations, I quickly learn that I find myself inadequate to resolve anything!

Sometimes it hits me in such a way that for a couple of days I may find myself in such a state that I feel numb at times. Here's the great part of it all, Jesus promised that He will never leave me nor forsake me! Though I was down and forgot who I was in Christ and felt the pressures, through it all, having a relationship with the Lord Jesus, the Spirit within me cries out and I am able to get back on board. One time it hit me to such an extent that this poem emerged:

Pressures come,

Pressures go

Pressures overflow

Family, church, me

Pressure, pressure you see

Pressure comes to me

Look to Jesus

And I will see

Pressure was never meant for me.

Cast your burdens

And your cares

Jesus said "I will bear"

Trust HIM always

Trust HIM today

Jesus will carry them all away!

It is so important to have a relationship with the Lord so that when difficult times come and though we may get down, or depressed we must at all times, in all situations and circumstances, we must look to JESUS! We must look to the Word of God! We must trust in the Lord! Proverbs 3:5,6 (NKJV) *"Trust in the Lord with all your heart, And lean not on your own understanding; In all your ways acknowledge Him, And He shall direct your paths."* I like how the Message Bible puts it: *"Trust God from the bottom of your heart; don't try to figure out everything on your own. Listen for God's voice in everything you do, everywhere you go; he's the one who will keep you on track. Don't assume that you know it all."*

Emphasis on the middle of the verses: *"...Listen for God's voice in everything you do, everywhere you go...."* This is critical in our walk with God! We must in our identification with Christ learn to listen for God's voice in everything we do and wherever we go! Again, because of life's situations and storms it is easily said than done! This is particularly true when we lean inward to find refuge and strength, instead of to our Heavenly Father who is not only our refuge and strength, but the very Source of life and provision. It's a process that we must go through. I have also learned that in going through these very real-life situations we also grow in our relationship with the Lord! We will get to know who HE is and in return we will discover who we are. I once heard it said this way, " *"If you take Christ from Christian you are left with "ian" which stands for* **'I ain't nothing without Christ!'** *"* Now, I don't know who first said it but I think it sums it all up for all of us who believe that after we give our lives to Christ we cannot go independent and live this life on our own! Friends, I have tried to do it on my own and found out rather quickly that IT DOESN'T WORK! I need to depend on the LORD at all times! It is during the times when I work independent of the Lord that I get myself into trouble. And consequently, I get depressed, worried, guilty, and shameful. I have a feeling that you have come to know what I am talking about! It is all because we think that we can handle it on our own. It is also during these times that God is there and telling us, *"let me handle it because I can!"* Jesus said it this way in Matthew

11:29: *Take my yoke upon you. Let me teach you, because I am humble and gentle at heart, and you will find rest for your souls. (NLT)* Again, I share with you the same passage from the Message Bible: *Are you tired? Worn out? Burned out on religion? Come to me. Get away with me and you'll recover your life. I'll show you how to take a real rest. Walk with me and work with me—watch how I do it. Learn the unforced rhythms of grace. I won't lay anything heavy or ill-fitting on you. Keep company with me and you'll learn to live freely and lightly.*

Saints, do not forget who you are in Christ Jesus! When those times come and you feel down and out, this is the time to get into the Word and remind yourself of who you are in Christ! It is in these times that you will find strength because you will be immersing yourself in the Word of God! I know that I must remind myself daily that in all things I need to look to the Lord! IN ALL THINGS!

Who are you? Repeat after me: I am a King's Kid! I have access to my Heavenly Father and I can go to Him at any time! I don't need a special invitation, or go through a secretary, or wait until the Lord is not busy – No, I can go to the Lord in prayer and He promises that He will answer when I call! I don't have to be anxious about anything because I know that my Heavenly Father hears me and knows me because I have a relationship with Him and I know who I am in Christ Jesus!

THE ENEMY'S PLOTTING AGAINST YOU

Now when the tempter came to Him, he said, "If You are the Son of God, command that these stones become bread."
Matthew 4:3 (NKJV)

In Matthew 4: 1-11 we find these words:

Then Jesus was led up by the Spirit into the wilderness to be tempted by the devil.[2] And when He had fasted forty days and forty nights, afterward He was hungry. [3] Now when the tempter came to Him, he said, "If You are the Son of God, command that these stones become bread." [4] But He answered said, "It is written, 'Man shall not live by bread alone, but by every word that proceeds from the mouth of God.'" [5] Then the devil took Him up into the holy city, set Him on the pinnacle of the temple, [6] and said to Him, "If You are the Son of God, throw Yourself down. For it is written: 'He shall give His angels charge over you,' and, 'In *their* hands they shall bear you up, Lest you dash your foot against a stone.'" [7] Jesus said to him, "It is written again, 'You shall not tempt the LORD your God.'" [8] Again, the devil took Him up on an exceedingly high mountain, and showed Him all the kingdoms of the world and their glory. [9] And he said to Him, "All these things I will give You if You will fall down and worship me." [10] Then Jesus said to him, "Away with you, Satan! For it is written, 'You shall worship the Lord your God, and Him only you shall serve.'" [11] Then the devil left Him, and behold, angels came and ministered to Him.

It is so interesting that first of all, all of this comes after Jesus' baptism and we hear the voice of the LORD saying to those who witnessed this event, "This is My beloved Son, in whom I am well pleased." Matt. 3:17(NKJV). The first thing that happens to Jesus is that the Spirit of the Living God leads Him to the wilderness to be tempted by the devil! Wow! God Himself led His Son to go face to face with the enemy! This was Jesus' preparation for what His Father had in store for Him to do while on this earth! There are many lessons for us to see and learn from this encounter between Jesus and Satan! If we pay close attention we will see that the enemy has not changed his tactics in trying to get to the people of GOD! I am so glad that Jesus is our example and shows us how to combat the enemy!

Had Jesus folded under the pressure and turned the bread to stones, jumped off the pinnacle, or accepting the kingdoms and glory of them and then bowed down to the enemy, Satan would have stolen the kingdom from Jesus, just as Satan took it from Adam in the garden – actually Adam handed it over to Satan because Adam forgot who he was in God! But Jesus did not fold under the pressure because He relied on the same Spirit that led Him into the wilderness with the purpose to be tempted by the devil! And it is the same Spirit of God that is available to the people of God today!

Jesus shows us how it is done by standing firm on the Word of God and obeying what it says! Each time Jesus would preference His statements with "It is written ....!" Let's take the cue from our example, Jesus, that this is how you defeat the enemy on every side! You stand on, you speak the Word of God in every situation in your life! The enemy will come after you especially when you declare to be saved or living for Jesus! You become Satan's public enemy number one! You are on his hit list! Reason being, Satan knows once you know the truth of your true identity that the kingdom of darkness is in trouble! Satan knows that defeat is upon him, her, it!

Satan will come to you when you are tired and hungry! Jesus had just come off a 40-day and 40-night fast! This was how the Spirit of the Lord led Him in the wilderness! All of what Jesus had to depend on was the fellowship and being in the presence of His Heavenly Father! Being that He came in the flesh, you know that the flesh was kicking up a storm to be fed, to be rested, to be taken care of to satisfy those needs! Through it all the Lord sustained Him during this period of time! Know that God was showing and building up in Jesus His identity! Showing Jesus what His assignment was for humanity! Jesus came to redeem humanity! If you think about it, that's a tall order and you must be ready for the onslaught of challenges coming from the kingdom of darkness who must indeed try to stop the "salvation of the Lord" from coming to humanity!

Satan will present dangerous shortcuts in your life to get you off focus of what God intends for your life! In this case with Jesus, Satan tried to sabotage Jesus' assignment by offering immediate satisfaction, fresh bread in seconds, a miraculous delivery, the kingdoms of the world and their glory! I read from the devotional "Our Daily Bread" commenting on this and the response from Jesus,

"But Jesus knew better. He knew that shortcuts were dangerous enemies. They may offer a road free from suffering, but in the end the pain they carry is much worse than anything we can imagine. "It is written," Jesus said three times

during His temptation. He held firm to what
He knew was true from God and His Word.
When we are tempted, God can help us too.
We can Depend on Him and the truth of His
Word to help us avoid dangerous shortcuts.
[Ochoa, Keila - OUR DAILY BREAD,
Dangerous Shortcuts, March 18, 2015].

And the devil is still doing the same thing on today
as back in the wilderness with Jesus – he is doing it
to the people of God by trying to get us off focus to
what God will have in our own lives by taking dangerous shortcuts! Face it, we do not want to go through
suffering or discomfort. If there is an easy way to
get it, we would rather take that road! This encounter
between Jesus and the devil lets us know that the easy
road is not the road we want to take! Yes, it would have
brought immediate relief to the flesh, but it would have
been costly spiritually as it was with Adam and Eve!

There are three lessons that I drew from this encounter between Jesus and the devil. Ponder them and gather the nuggets you need to know who you are.

Lesson 1: The enemy will always challenge you as to your true identity! How many of us have been challenged after we have given our lives to the Lord? Family and friends would come up to you, knowing you from the past and would indeed challenge you as to the authenticity of your salvation in Christ Jesus! They cannot see you beyond what you were! They remember the old times in which you would hang out with them and for some, it was partying together, drinking together, drugging, fornicating, cussing, robbing, all sorts of evil and unlawful things, now you are saying to me that you are now "saved?" Yes, the enemy will come after you through those that you thought would never question your new walk in the Lord!

Know that the enemy will also come to you when you are tired and hungry! Also, when you seem confused and wondering what is going on! I can remember in my own life and it just seem as if the LORD was not listening to my prayers. I was in a wilderness! Then I began questioning the Lord and I asked the Lord, "Lord, do you still love me? Am I the man of God you have called me to be?" I was really doubting of who I was in the Lord! God has a way of indeed sending an answer in different ways! I am sure you have your moments of being down and wondering if the Lord loved you or not or why has He led you to the "wilderness!" In my case the Lord answered by sending a person I hadn't seen in several years. When we saw each other he was with another person and the words that came out of his mouth by way of introducing me to the other person were the words I needed to hear and knowing that it was the Lord speaking to my heart and spirit – he said, "...I want you to meet a man of God

...." Oh, how those words simply bless my heart and from that point on, for that season I was able to continue on and it brought me out of the wilderness.

Jesus came out of that first round with the enemy by saying, "It is written, 'Man shall not live by bread alone, but by every word that proceeds from the mouth of God.'" In other words, for us as a believer, it is imperative that we know what GOD says about who we are! We are in trouble if when the enemy comes in and challenges us that we fold under the pressure and we begin to doubt who we are in Christ Jesus! This is when we must know what God's Word is saying as to who we are! Jesus did not hesitate because He was the Word who became flesh and dwelt among the people! Jesus is our example! So, in this first lesson know that the enemy will challenge your true identity! We must be strong in the faith and let that enemy know – I live by the Word of God! I am who God says I am!

Lesson 2: The enemy will challenge your true identity by asking you to do something to prove that you are who you say you are.

Satan will want you to prove that you are who you say you are by tempting you to do something that is in the Word of God. Here the enemy will get crafty on you and ask you to prove that the Word of God is true! Since Jesus used scripture in the first round, the enemy used scripture to try and deceive Jesus in shortcutting His assignment! Satan tried to get Jesus to commit suicide, all to prove that the angels would come and rescue him before he hit the ground! Just as in the garden with Adam and Eve observe the cunning words as recorded in Matthew 4:6, *6 and said to Him, "If You are the Son of God, throw Yourself down. For it is written: 'He shall give His angels charge over you,' and, 'In their hands they shall bear you up, Lest you dash your foot against a stone.'"* The enemy is challenging Jesus to commit suicide to see or to prove whether or not the Word of

God is true and have Jesus prove that He was the Son of God. Had Jesus jumped, he would have obeyed the request of the enemy. This was a trick of the enemy to have Jesus to so call prove to Satan of who He is. Jesus responded using the Word and said, *"It is written again, 'You shall not tempt the LORD your God.'"*

This is how you do it my friends! You grab hold of the Word of God and you commit it to your life's living standing firm upon it as you face each day, each challenge, each problem or situation! It is the Word of God that will keep you out of trouble and from not sinning! The Psalmist put it this way: *Thy word have I hid in mine heart, that I might not sin against thee. Psalms 119:11 (NKJV).*

People of God do not fall for the trap the enemy has laid up for you by challenging you to prove that you are a child of God! You don't have to prove, all you need to do is live it! Live according to what the Word of God guides and directs you to do!

Lesson 3: The enemy will promise the "world" to you in exchange to worship him.

In our society today fame and fortune is a goal that most Americans seek after. Well, the enemy knows this and it is nothing new that there are so many things especially in the United States that will promote a quick fix of gaining fame and fortune! These are dangerous shortcuts and it all stems from not knowing who you are in the Lord! Many think that if they were to hit the lottery that then all their worries and concern will be over! Sure you will have the money to pay off your bills, debts, and may not have to worry about money again but if you don't have the wisdom of God or you forget the Lord in this new found wealth, then before you know it you will have lost all that money because you did not acknowledge God and will spend it on your own lust in addition to, find holes in your pockets! Haggai gives this warning: *You have planted much but harvest little. You eat but are not satisfied. You drink but are still thirsty.*

You put on clothes but cannot keep warm. Your wages disappear as though you were putting them in pockets filled with holes! Haggai 1:6 (NLT). This the prophet said because the people of God left the house of God in ruins and were more concerned with their own houses! This will happen when we don't consider the Lord in our hearts and plans!

The enemy will indeed promise you many things, but don't think that he will deliver on any of those things! The bottom line to it all is that Satan does not have it to give, because it belong to Jesus from the very beginning. Jesus has taken it back from his hands! When Jesus conquered the grave and rose triumphantly, that secured our victory! The resurrection placed everything back into the hands of the people of God! Now it is up to the people of God to know who they are in Christ Jesus and begin to fulfil that Kingdom Mandate and to live from victory to victory claiming all that Jesus have obtained for the believers!

People of God the enemy is plotting against us, but just as Jesus proved that if you stand firm on the Word of God and you speak the Word of God to your situations, then the same results will come to you as it did for Jesus as you invoke the authority and dominion you have over the enemy, *Then Jesus said to him, "Away with you, Satan! For it is written, 'You shall worship the Lord your God, and Him only you shall serve.'"* *[11] Then the devil left Him, and behold, angels came and ministered to Him.* You can speak to the enemy and tell him he has to leave. Afterwards go worship the LORD and serve HIM! You make your stand, and the angels of the LORD will come and minister to you and strengthen you to stand!

The enemy will plot, but the plot will not prosper, it will not come to pass if you know who you are! Who are you?

FALSE IDENTITY

"...among whom also we all once conducted our-
selves in the lusts of our flesh, fulfilling the desires
of the flesh and of the mind, and were by nature
children of wrath, just as the others."
Ephesians 2:3 (NKJV)

believe people who do wrong or go against the Word of God are those who have not encountered the Lord Jesus Christ or have decided to live this "false identity" given to them by the devil. I say false identity because that is not who God made you and I to be! You have been created into the image and likeness of God! Yes, now, since Adam and Eve disobeyed we were born in iniquity and our identity was stolen from us. Sin entered the world and since that time we as humans have been doing our own thing and unfortunately for the most part, things that are and were displeasing to God.

Cain killed his brother Abel! Why? Because he acted in a rage of jealousy because his offering was not accepted by the Lord! Why did the Lord reject Cain's offering? There are several reasons debated by bible scholars: God's Sovereign choice, non-blood Sacrifice, poor quality, attitude problem and choice of occupation. I reject the notion of non-blood sacrifice because it wasn't a sacrifice they made to the Lord it was an offering! And choice of occupation I don't agree with because then that would make the Lord partial to certain occupations in this case a shepherd Abel (…a keeper of sheep (Genesis 4:2b)) over a farmer Cain, (… a tiller of the ground (Genesis 4:2c)). God desires that in all that we say and do, we do to His glory no matter what occupation we may undertake. In all things that take place the Sovereignty of God is at work! This simply means that God does what HE wants to do and does not need to explain Himself! Who am I to contest what GOD does? Job himself experienced this first-hand about questioning God. After his encounter with God and God asking him some questions Job speaks,

"I am nothing—how could I ever find the answers? I will cover my mouth with my hand. ⁵ I have said too much already. I have nothing more to say.... Then Job replied to the LORD: ² "I know that you can do anything, and no one can stop you. ³ You asked, 'Who is this that questions my wisdom with such ignorance?' It is I—and I was talking about things I knew nothing about, things far too wonderful for

me. **⁴You said, 'Listen and I will speak! I have some questions for you, and you must answer them.' ⁵I had only heard about you before, but now I have seen you with my own eyes. ⁶I take back everything I said, and I sit in dust and ashes to show my repentance." Job 40:4-5; 42:1-6, NLT**

Since HE is Sovereign, He can do whatever He pleases. Contrary to popular belief – GOD IS IN CONTROL! HE WAS NEVER OUT OF CONTROL! So definitely, God's Sovereignty is always at work, but for our sake and purpose of this book, I want to offer and accept the notion that Cain's offering was rejected because of poor quality and attitude! These reasons can help us in our understanding of who we are! I believe that Cain did not bring the best offering! I believe at the time of offering unto the Lord, Cain brought the fruits that had already fallen off the trees.

Bruised and damaged, maybe even bitten off by animals or the birds! As a boy I picked pears for my mother so that she can bottle them in the Mason jars and make pear pies later or share them with others! It was so much easier to pick them up off the ground, but the majority of those pears on the ground were either bruised, eaten by the birds or worm invested. To get the best pears, I had to climb the pear tree and pick them off the branches so I believe Cain made it easy for himself and picked up the poor quality of his fruit off the ground.

On the heels of not taking any thought of what to give unto the Lord, comes the attitude behind giving. I believe Cain's attitude behind his giving was one of "this will do!" Attitude determines our altitude in God! If our attitude is not right with our giving, then we are truly fooling ourselves into thinking that it is acceptable before God! God is concerned more about the condition of our heart then about what we are giving! Don Stewart writes:

"…God was not so much concerned with the type of sacrifice or the quality of the offering. They contend that His main concern was with the attitude of Cain. Cain's offering was rejected because of his impure heart, not because it was the fruit of the land rather than a blood sacrifice. He may have brought the very best that he had, but he did so with entirely the wrong attitude. This would be comparable to somebody giving a large sum of money to the church with a grudging attitude." (Stewart, D. (24 Apr, 2007). Why Did God Reject Cain's Sacrifice?. Retrieved from https://www.blueletterbible.org/faq/don_stewart/don_stewart_714.cfm).

The Apostle Paul wrote to the people at Corinth when talking about giving to the Lord: ***"You must each decide in your heart how much to give. And don't give reluctantly or in response to pressure.***

"For God loves a person who gives cheerfully." II Corinthians 9:7 (GWT)

The message for each of us is that when we don't walk in our true identity, but a false identity it will cause us to not give our very best with an attitude of "this will do!"

Under the Uniform Code of Military Justice (UCMJ) Article 133 - Conduct unbecoming an officer and gentleman, an officer in the military can be charged when certain offenses are carried out. Instances of violation of this article include: knowingly making a false official statement; dishonorable failure to pay a debt; cheating on an exam; opening and reading a letter of another without authority; using insulting or defamatory language to another officer in that officer's presence or about that officer to other military persons; being drunk and disorderly in a public place; public association with known prostitutes; committing or attempting to commit a crime involving moral turpitude; and failing without good cause to support the officer's family. *(Powers, Rod (08 Sep 2016). Punitive Articles of the UCMJ: Article 133 – Conduct unbecoming an officer and gentleman. Retrieved from https://www.the balance.com/ punitive-articles-of-the-ucmj-3356843).* These occur when the person forgets who they are when wearing the uniform or even out of the uniform. It's not what you wear on the outside that makes you, but it is what's on the inside. The proverb writer said, ***"As in water face reflects face, So a man's heart reveals the man." Proverb 27:19 (NKJV).*** What's in your heart? When the enemy steals our identity or we fall prey to the lies, it opens the door for our hearts to be invaded by "stinkin thinkin!" We will begin to think that we can get away with doing wrong! Most importantly, we think that perhaps we can get one over on God. Our hearts will be turned from God! Therefore, we will do things unbecoming of our true identity which is that we have been made in the image and likeness of God!

BUT GOD has made a way to recapture your true identity! Remember what God said to the serpent in Genesis 3:15 – *"And I will put enmity between you and the woman, and between your seed and her Seed; He shall bruise your head, And you shall bruise His heel." (NKJV).* God's design and way is capsulated in John 3:16, *For God so loved the world that He gave His only begotten Son, that whoever believes in Him should not perish but have everlasting life.* God's beacon of light for humankind to return to their true identity is to establish a relationship with Jesus Christ, the Lamb of God, the perfect sacrifice. When Jesus entered Jerusalem during the final week on earth, the people gathered and cheered, *"So they took palm branches and went to meet him. They were shouting, "Hosanna! Blessed is the one who comes in the name of the Lord, the king of Israel!"" John 12:13, (GWT).* Jesus Christ was and is the Savior of the world and the only one that can give us back our true identity. It is only through a relationship with the Lord Jesus Christ and giving ourselves to His rulership and authority that the true and real identity of who we are will be revealed. What God says who we are according to His Word and our relationship through Jesus Christ answers the question: Who Are You?

WHO ARE YOU? THIS IS WHO YOU ARE

Ye are of God, little children, and have overcome them: because greater is he that is in you, than he that is in the world.

I John 4:4, KJV

*T*he Word of God helps us and reminds us of who we are in Christ Jesus! It is important for each of us to confess the truth of God's Word over our lives as well as to remind those who have given themselves to the Lord Jesus Christ and are born again. It is important that you understand that it is your "spirit"

that is born again! In John 3 there is this conversation
with a ruler of the Jews who came to Jesus by night:

[1] There was a man of the Pharisees named
Nicodemus, a ruler of the Jews. [2] This man
came to Jesus by night and said to Him,
"Rabbi, we know that You are a teacher come
from God; for no one can do these signs
that You do unless God is with him." [3] Jesus
answered and said to him, "Most assuredly, I
say to you, unless one is born again, he cannot
see the kingdom of God." [4] Nicodemus said
to Him, "How can a man be born when he is
old? Can he enter a second time into his mother's womb and be born?" [5] Jesus answered,
"Most assuredly, I say to you, unless one is
born of water and the Spirit, he cannot enter
the kingdom of God. [6] That which is born of
the flesh is flesh, and that which is born of

the Spirit is spirit. [7] Do not marvel that I said

to you, 'You must be born again.' [8] The wind

blows where it wishes, and you hear the sound

of it, but cannot tell where it comes from and

where it goes. So is everyone who is born of

the Spirit." John 3:1-8 (NKJV)

Therefore, though your flesh continues to fight

against the redeemed, the saved Spirit that is in you

when you received Jesus as your Lord and Savior, you

must confess who you are in Christ Jesus "...because

greater is He that is in you, than he that is in the world."

1 John 4:4 (KJV)

So, to reclaim your true identity in Christ, you must

first be born again. Read the following scriptures and

believe that GOD is talking to you directly, because He

is! Open your heart to these scriptures, confess that

you are a sinner and receive Jesus Christ as your Lord

and Savior! This is the way to be saved, redeemed and to reclaim your true identity. Follow these steps:

1. **Know that God loves you.** John 3:16, (NLT) *"For this is how God loved the world: He gave his one and only Son, so that everyone who believes in him will not perish but have eternal life.* And also Romans 5:8, (AMPC), *But God shows and clearly proves His [own] love for us by the fact that while we were still sinners, Christ (the Messiah, the Anointed One) died for us.*

2. **Agree that before Christ entered in our lives we are all sinners.** Romans 3:10, (NKJV), *As it is written: "There is none righteous, no, not one;....* And Romans 3:23 (NLT), *For everyone has sinned; we all fall short of God's glorious standard.*

3. **Know that God has a remedy for sin**. John 1:12, (AMPC) *But to as many as did*

receive and welcome Him, He gave the authority (power, privilege, right) to become the children of God, that is, to those who believe in (adhere to, trust in, and rely on) His name. Romans 6:23, (ERV), *When people sin, they earn what sin pays—death. But God gives his people a free gift—eternal life in Christ Jesus our Lord.* And I Corinthians 15:3-4, (NKJV), *For I delivered to you first of all that which I also received: that Christ died for our sins according to the Scriptures, [4] and that He was buried, and that He rose again the third day according to the Scriptures, ….*

4. **Believe that now is the day of salvation, you can be saved right now.** Romans 10:13, (NKJV), *For "whoever calls on the name of the LORD shall be saved."*

Revelations 3:20, (NLT), *"Look! I stand at the door and knock. If you hear my voice and open the door, I will come in, and we will share a meal together as friends.*

If you have followed the steps to be saved and today was your day, record it and remember this day because it is the greatest day of your life. Welcome to the family! I am rejoicing with you of your salvation! Not only me, but all of heaven is rejoicing right now because of your decision to follow Jesus Christ. Luke 15:7 (NLT) *In the same way, there is more joy in heaven over one lost sinner who repents and returns to God than over ninety-nine others who are righteous and haven't strayed away!* And verse 10 says, *In the same way, there is joy in the presence of God's angels when even one sinner repents."*

If you had already made the decision to follow Christ, but you may have fallen away, reclaim the scriptures just read and begin living again confidently that Jesus is in your life! Reassure yourselves with the following scriptures: John 5:24, (ERV), *"I assure you, anyone who hears what I say and believes in the one who sent me has eternal life. They will not be judged guilty. They have already left death and have entered into life...."* John 20:31, (AMPC), *But these are written (recorded) in order that you may believe that Jesus is the Christ (the Anointed One), the Son of God, and that through believing and cleaving to and trusting and relying upon Him you may have life through (in) His name [through Who He is].* Romans 10:9, (NLT), *If you openly declare that Jesus is Lord and believe in your heart that God raised him from the dead, you will be saved.* And I John 5:13, (ERV), *I write this letter to you who believe in the Son of God. I write so that you will know that you have eternal life now.*

Now that you have the foundation, you are ready to discover your Kingdom Identity. Confess the following and speak into your life the I AMs' and study the scriptures to get it in your Spirit! Know them for yourself so that you will not be deceived by the enemy. After each affirmation write out how it speaks to you. Study the scriptures which informs you of who you are in Christ!

I am: God's child for I am born again of the incorruptible seed of the Word of God. 1 Peter 1:23. _____

_____

_____

_____

_____

_____

I am: Forgiven of all my sins and washed in the Blood. Ephesians 1:7, Hebrews 9:14, Colossians 1:14, 1 John 1:9.

_____

_____

_____

_____

_____

I am: A new creature in Christ. 2 Corinthians 5:17.

_____

_____

_____

_____

_____

I am: The temple of the Holy Spirit. 1 Corinthians 6:19.

_____

_____

_____

_____

_____

I am: Delivered from the power of darkness and translated in God's kingdom. Colossians 1:13.

_____

_____

_____

_____

_____

I am: Given the Holy Spirit as a pledge, a guarantee of my inheritance. Ephesians 1:13-14.

_____

_____

_____

_____

_____

I am: Crucified with Christ and it is no longer I who lives, but Christ. Galatians 2:20. _____

_____

_____

_____

_____

_____

I am: Redeemed from the curse of the law of sin and death. 1 Peter 1:18-19, Galatians 3:13.

_____

_____

_____

_____

_____

I am: Blessed. Deuteronomy 28:2-12, Galatians 3:9.

_____

_____

_____

_____

_____

I am: The Elect of God. Colossians 3:12, Romans 8:33.

_____

_____

_____

_____

I am: Established to the end. Romans 1:11.

_____

_____

_____

_____

_____

I am: Made near to My Heavenly Father by the Blood of Christ. Ephesians 2:13.

_____

_____

_____

_____

_____

_____

_____

I am: Set free. John 8:31-33.

_____

_____

_____

_____

_____

I am: Strong in the Lord. Ephesians 6:10.

_____

_____

_____

_____

_____

_____

_____

I am: Dead to sin. Romans 6:1, 11 and 1 Peter 2:24.

_____

_____

_____

_____

_____

I am: A Saint. Romans 1:7, 1 Corinthians 1:2, Philippians 1:1.

_____

_____

_____

_____

_____

I am: The head and not the tail, above and not beneath. Deuteronomy 28:13.

_____

_____

_____

_____

_____

I am: Holy and without blame before Him in love. 1 Peter 1:16, Ephesians 1:4

_____

_____

_____

_____

_____

I am: More than a conqueror. Romans 8:37.

_____

_____

_____

_____

_____

I am: Joint heir with Christ. Romans 8:13.

_____

_____

_____

_____

_____

I am: Sealed with the Holy Spirit of promise. Ephesians 1:13.

_____

_____

_____

_____

_____

I am: In Christ by His doing. 1 Corinthians 1:30.

_____

_____

_____

_____

_____

I am: Accepted in the Beloved. Ephesians 1:6.

_____

_____

_____

_____

_____

I am: Complete in Him. Colossians 2:10.

_____

_____

_____

_____

_____

I am: Crucified and Alive with Christ. Galatians 2:20.

_____

_____

_____

_____

_____

I am: Free from condemnation. John 5:24.

_____

_____

_____

_____

_____

I am: Reconciled to God. 2 Corinthians 5:18

_____

_____

_____

_____

_____

I am: Qualified to share in His inheritance. Colossians 1:12.

_____

_____

_____

_____

_____

I am: Firmly rooted, built up, established in my faith and overflowing with thanksgiving. Colossians 2:7.

_____

_____

_____

_____

_____

I am: Born of God and the evil one does not touch me. 1 John 5:18.

_____

_____

_____

_____

_____

I am: His faithful follower. Revelation 17:14, Ephesians 5:1.

_____

_____

_____

_____

I am: A fellow citizen with the saints of the household of God. Ephesians 2:19.

_____

_____

_____

_____

_____

I am: His disciple because I have love for others. John 13:34-35.

_____

_____

_____

_____

_____

I am: The light of the world. Matthew 5:14

_____

_____

_____

_____

_____

I am: The salt of the earth. Matthew 5:13.

_____

_____

_____

_____

_____

I am: Built upon the foundation of the apostles and prophets, Jesus Christ Himself being the chief corner stone. Ephesians 2:20.

_____

_____

_____

_____

_____

I am: Overtaken with blessings. Deuteronomy 28:2 and Ephesians 1:3.

_____

_____

_____

_____

_____

I am: The righteousness of God. 2 Corinthians 5:21, 1 Peter 2:24

_____

_____

_____

_____

_____

I am: A partaker of His Divine Nature. 2 Peter 1:4.

_____

_____

_____

_____

_____

I am: Called of God. 2 Timothy 1:9.

_____

_____

_____

_____

_____

I am: An ambassador for Christ. 2 Corinthians 5:20

_____

_____

_____

_____

_____

I am: God's workmanship created in Christ Jesus for good works. Ephesians 2:10.

_____

_____

_____

_____

_____

I am: The apple of my Father's eye. Deuteronomy 32:10.

_____

_____

_____

_____

_____

I am: Healed by the stripes of Jesus. 1 Peter 2:24, Isaiah

53:5 _____

_____

_____

_____

_____

_____

I am: Being changed into His image. 2 Corinthians 3:18, Philippians 1:6

_____

_____

_____

_____

_____

I am: A child of God. John 1:12, Romans 8:16.

_____

_____

_____

_____

_____

I am: Christ's friend. John 15:15.

_____

_____

_____

_____

_____

I am: Chosen and appointed by Christ to bear His fruit.
John 15:16.

_____

_____

_____

_____

_____

I am: A slave of righteousness. Romans 6:16.

_____

_____

_____

_____

_____

I am: Enslaved to God. Romans 6:22.

_____

_____

_____

_____

_____

I am: A son/daughter of God. Romans 8:14-15, Galatians 3:26 and 4:6.

_____

_____

_____

_____

_____

I am: A temple of God, His Spirit dwells in me. 1 Corinthians 3:16, 6:19

_____

_____

_____

_____

_____

I am: Joined to the Lord and I am one with him. 1 Corinthians 6:17

_____

_____

_____

_____

_____

I am: A member of Christ's Body. 1 Corinthians 12:27, Ephesians 5:30.

_____

_____

_____

_____

_____

I am: Reconciled to God and I am a minister of reconciliation. 2 Corinthians 5:18-19

_____

_____

_____

_____

_____

I am: One in Christ. Galatians 3:26, 28.

_____

_____

_____

_____

_____

I am: An heir of God since I am a son/daughter of God. Galatians 4:6-7.

_____

_____

_____

_____

_____

I am: Righteous and holy. Ephesians 4:24.

_____

_____

_____

_____

_____

I am: A citizen of Heaven and seated in Heaven. Philippians 3:20, Ephesians 2:6.

_____

_____

_____

_____

_____

I am: An expression of the Life of Christ because He is my life. Colossians 3:4.

_____

_____

_____

_____

_____

I am: Chosen and dearly loved by Christ. Ephesians 1:4, 1 Peter 2:9.

_____

_____

_____

_____

_____

I am: A son/daughter of light and not of darkness. 1 Thessalonians 5:5.

_____

_____

_____

_____

_____

I am: A Holy brother/sister, partaker of a Heavenly Calling. Hebrews 3:1

_____

_____

_____

_____

_____

I am: One of God's living stones and I am being brought up as a spiritual house. 1 Peter 2:5

_____

_____

_____

_____

_____

I am: A Chosen Race, a Royal Priesthood, a Holy Nation, a people for God's own possession to proclaim the excellence of Him. 1 Peter 2:9-10.

_____

_____

_____

_____

_____

I am: An alien and stranger to this world I temporarily live in. 1 Peter 2:11.

_____

_____

_____

_____

_____

I am: The enemy of the Devil. 1 Peter 5:8.

_____

_____

_____

_____

_____

I am: Now a child of God, I will resemble Christ when He returns. 1 John 3:1-2.

_____

_____

_____

_____

_____

I am: Not the great I AM but by the grace of God I am what I am because of God's favor. 1 Corinthians 15:10.

_____

_____

_____

_____

_____

I am: Made righteous. Romans 5:1.

_____

_____

_____

_____

_____

I am: Dead with Christ and dead to the power of sin's rule over my life. Romans 6:1-6.

_____

_____

_____

_____

_____

I am: Dead, I no longer live for myself but for God. 2 Corinthians 5:14-15

_____

_____

_____

_____

_____

I am: Bought with a price, I am not my own, I belong to God. 1 Corinthians 6:19-20

_____

_____

_____

_____

_____

I am: Established, anointed and sealed by God in Christ. 2 Corinthians 1:21-22

_____

_____

_____

_____

_____

Do you see now why the enemy's task and purpose is to steal the people of God's identity? The enemy is in trouble when the child of God realizes who he/she is in Christ! When you walk in your true identity, the enemy cannot pull the wool over your eyes for your spirit will detect the devil's activities. When you walk in your true identity, you will know what is yours and that you have dominion, an inheritance, life and peace! You will begin to live that abundant life as promised in John 10:10, *A thief comes to steal, kill, and destroy. But I came so that my sheep will have life and so that they will have everything they need. (GWT)*

CONCLUSION

"Behold, I am coming quickly! Blessed is he who
keeps the words of the prophecy of this book."
Revelation 22:7

here was an interesting occurrence that took place in the garden where they arrested Jesus. It is only recorded in the book of John: *Jesus therefore, knowing all things that would come upon Him, went forward and said to them, "Whom are you seeking?" ⁵ They answered Him, "Jesus of Nazareth." Jesus said to them, "I am He." And Judas, who betrayed Him, also stood with them. ⁶ Now when He said to them, "I am He," they drew back and fell to the ground. John 18:4-6, (NKJV).*

Did you catch it? It is verse 6, *Now when He said to them, "I am He," they drew back and fell to the ground.* Wait a minute. Jesus said "I am He" and they fell to the ground! Wow, what power. It did not say that Jesus hit them, ambushed them, nor raised His hand, He simply said, "I AM HE" and they fell to the ground! Matthew Henry's commentary on this verse excited me and was so rich to me I have to share it with you. He said, "

See how he terrified them, and obliged them to retire (<u>John 18:6</u>): They went backward, and, like men thunder-struck, fell to the ground. It should seem, they did not fall forward, as humbling themselves before him, and yielding to him, but backward, as standing it out to the utmost. Thus Christ

*was declared to be more than a man, even
when he was trampled upon as a worm, and
no man. This word, I am he, had revived his
disciples, and raised them up (<u>Matt. 14:27</u>);
but the same word strikes his enemies down.
Hereby he showed plainly, (1.) What he
could have done with them. When he struck
them down, he could have struck them dead;
when he spoke them to the ground, he could
have spoken them to hell, ... but he would
not do so, ...*

Isn't that an awesome commentary? Jesus spoke
His true identity, I AM HE! It evokes power and Jesus
identifies Himself with His Heavenly Father who spoke
to Moses in the desert when Moses asked the question,
*"Then Moses said to God, "Suppose I go to the People
of Israel and I tell them, 'The God of your fathers
sent me to you'; and they ask me, 'What is his name?'*

What do I tell them?" [14] *God said to Moses, "I-AM-WHO-I-AM. Tell the People of Israel, 'I-AM sent me to you.'" Exodus 3:13-14 (MSG)).*

In the preceding chapter, there are a series of confessions answering the question "Who Are You," each starting with "I AM!" Friends there is power and authority in invoking who you are and revealing your true identity! I am convinced that the more we confess it and speak it over our lives, the more we become what we say. In the New King James Version (NKJV) Genesis chapter one, verses 3, 6, 9, 11, 14, 20, 24, and 26 they all begin the same way, *"And God said, ..."* God would go on to say what He had to say and at the end of whatever God said, verses 7, 9, 11, 15, 24 and 30 you have a recurring *"... and it was so."* This tells me that whenever God says something it came to pass! Now, let me remind you that we are living breathing representations of God because we have been made in His image and likeness. Therefore, we have the same creative powers that when we say something, IT IS SO! Therefore, when we confess what God says from His Word of who we are, then IT IS SO!

Gospel recording artist Donald Lawrence penned these words in his song *"There Is A King In You"* that I believe is a fitting ending and conclusion to what I want to encourage you all within answering the question "Who Are You?" Donald Lawrence wrote:

You come from Royalty,

An aristocratic dynasty.

The goal of the enemy,

Is that you don't know who you are.

There's power when you speak.

Be mindful of words you release.

I know that life has challenged you,

But the King in me speaks to the King in you.

You were born to rule.

There is a king in you.

(Lawrence, Donald (January 30, 2009, Zomba Recording LLC).
There Is a King in You. Retrieved from http:// www.azlyrics.com/lyrics/donaldlawrence/ thereisakinginyou.html)

These words I pray will embolden you to go out and be all that you can be in the name of the Lord and to live out your true identity in the Lord! Answer the question with boldness. Who are you? Boldly proclaim what is on the inside of you man, woman, declare I AM A KING!!

f

CPSIA information can be obtained
at www.ICGtesting.com
Printed in the USA
BVHW040315261218
536333BV00010B/600/P

9 781545 619285